~~Worthing~~

~~HN~~
SS

Kleinwort
Arguity
11/11

GW00566606

West Sussex County Council Library

Please return/renew this item by the last
date shown. Books may also be renewed
by phone 01243 642110 or the Internet.

www.westsussex.gov.uk

west
sussex
county
council

200726514

Selima Hill grew up in a family of painters in farms in England and Wales, and has lived in Dorset for the past 20 years. She won first prize in the Arvon/*Observer* International Poetry Competition with part of *The Accumulation of Small Acts of Kindness* (1989), one of several extended sequences in *Gloria: Selected Poems* (Bloodaxe Books, 2008). *Gloria* includes work from *Saying Hello at the Station* (1984), *My Darling Camel* (1988), *A Little Book of Meat* (1993), *Aeroplanes of the World* (1994), *Violet* (1997), *Bunny* (2001), *Portrait of My Lover as a Horse* (2002), *Lou-Lou* (2004) and *Red Roses* (2006). Her latest collections from Bloodaxe are *The Hat* (2008) and *Fruit-cake* (2009).

Violet was a Poetry Book Society Choice and was short-listed for all three of the UK's major poetry prizes, the Forward Prize, T.S. Eliot Prize and Whitbread Poetry Award. *Bunny* won the Whitbread Poetry Award, was a Poetry Book Society Choice and was shortlisted for the T.S. Eliot Prize. *Lou-Lou* and *The Hat* were Poetry Book Society Recommendations. She was given a Cholmondeley Award in 1986, and was a Royal Literary Fund Fellow at the University of Exeter in 2003-06.

Selima Hill reads a half-hour selection of her poems on *The Poetry Quartets: 2* (Bloodaxe Books/The British Council, 1998), a double-cassette shared with Fleur Adcock, Carol Ann Duffy and Carol Rumens.

As a tutor, Selima Hill has worked in prisons, hospitals and monasteries as well as for the Arvon Foundation and London's South Bank Centre. She has worked on several collaborations with artists including: *Parched Swallows* with choreographer Emily Claid; *Point of Entry* with sculptor Bill Woodrow; and *Trembling Hearts in the Bodies of Rocks* with performance artist Ilona Medved-Lost.

SELIMA HILL

FRUITCAKE

BLOODAXE BOOKS

Copyright © Selima Hill

ISBN: 978 1 85224 848

First published 2009 by
Bloodaxe Books Ltd,
Highgreen,
Tarset,
Northumberland NE48 11

www.bloodaxebooks.com
For further information about Bloodaxe titles
please visit our website or write to
the above address for a catalogue.

Bloodaxe Books Ltd acknowledges
the financial assistance of
Arts Council England, North East.

Cover design: Neil Astley & Pamela Robertson-Pearce.

Printed in Great Britain by
Bell & Bain Limited, Glasgow, Scotland.

CONTENTS

NYLON

BOUGAINVILLEA

Bones

In the hot
benighted nursing-home

machines like cats
blink beside the beds

of bony babies
nurses rarely handle.

With My Body Bespangled

With my body bespangled with house-flies
like precious jewels,

with my naked body
bespangled by ardent house-flies

like precious jewels
flung from the turrets of castles

by furious hands
with filth-encrusted fingernails,

I lie in my snow-white cot
on my snow-white linens

and abandon myself
to my long contamination.

The King

Every day
the largest fly in Christendom

walks across my head
like a king

walking out
across a crust of sand

in which he dreams
his own true love lies bleeding.

For Ever

The flies that mill around my cot
are whimpering

that, even if they stay with me all
all summer,

crawling on my face
and in my hair

and in my mouth
and up and down my ears,

they'll never get enough of me;
they whisper

they want my wounds
to weep for them for ever!

Pilots

They worship at the altar of my flesh
like tiny pilots who have lost their minds

and worship me by sitting on my head:
they've come so far they'll worship anything!

O look at this, they can't believe their luck –
so raw, so juicy, so convenient!

All they have to do is to pick their way
across a slough of Vaseline and Calamine

until they reach a sort of succulent plateau
where *everything* has been *laid out* for them.

Roses

Roses shimmer
and my warm machinery

twinkles round my head
like pearls and diamonds

twinkling
in the balconies of heaven

where saints in white
look down on me sternly.

Herself

I watch the fly,
attracted by my wounds,

obstinately
quartering my net;

and when the fly
tiptoes out of sight

I watch the distant outline
of my mother

who likes to keep herself
to herself.

Euphoria

Euphoric flies
collide with the sun

that's battering the lawn
where my mother

creeps towards me
like a creeping hat.

Pram

When my mother
sees what she has done

she rolls me in a blanket
like a thumb

and props me in a pram
in the sun

but no, I'm much too sick
to be well

and have to be unwrapped again
and fanned.

Sunlight

Sunlight fills my pram
like a butcher

who peels shrimp
and turns them inside out

and pinches them
between his golden fingernails

and crunches them
between his golden teeth:

it fills the pram
and gilds the little addicts

that mill about
the dunes of my net.

Heat May Blind

Heat may blind the nurse
but not the flies

that creep about
in search of the secretions

that sparkle on my head
like pink and gold

jewels
in an extraterrestrial jewellery shop.

The Sun

The sun is hot
and a large fly

flies into the pram,
then buzzes off,

only to return
minutes later

as if by now
it is a friend of mine.

Nervousness

Anything alive
makes her nervous –

visitors, their flowers,
the endless flies,

and, dying
in my little muslin living-room,

me
and my unmanageable head.

To Flies My Head

To flies, my head
is like a dead fish

on which to gorge
before staggering off.

Mouse

When Mother thinks,
her little grey-brown heart

forgets
what it's supposed to be doing:

imagine she's a mouse
one can't expect

to feed me
and fan me all the time.

Black Against the Copper

Black against the copper
bourgainvillea bracts

that push against the brickwork,
flies are gathering:

from every crack and crevice
they are watching

as someone props a baby
on a bed –

the sickest
and most succulent little baby

it's ever been their privilege
to sip at.

My Mother's Blouse

In my mother's blouse
my mother's breasts,

as cold as stone,
withhold my warm milk.

Dressing-gown

I stain the cot,
I stain the large bra,

I stain the faded
gold and silver dressing-gown

which may be very lovely
but can't help.

My Mother's Hen

A baby like a rock with no arms
has suddenly been placed in her bed,

a rock she sprinkles nervously with handkerchiefs
in order to disguise it as a hen.

The Mole

The panic-stricken mole
with hands like wood

who seems to be confused
by the light

that clatters through the plastic blinds
like mussel shells

is actually
my panic-stricken mother!

God

God shakes a drop of milk
from her nipple

into His enormous hand
and licks it:

just because she says
she doesn't like me

she mustn't think
He's going to take me back!

The Pigeon

I'm lying in my pram
in the shade

like cheeses
set to cool in a larder,

protected from the flies
by my net

and by a pigeon
from the sound of wheezing.

Ponies

Her lonely days and nights
pass like ponies

eating flowers
by the railway

where trains go hurtling by
and hit the ponies

but no one cares
because they're not their ponies!

Rain

Rain is falling
on a million trees

and on the links
and on the waterfalls

and on the house
in whose palatial drawing-room

she hears a buzzing
from inside my shawl.

Sugar

She flicks the grains of sugar
off my cheek

with hands like lizards
darting out of walls.

Bluebottles

They make their way in haste
to my head

up snowy glens,
helpless with gratitude.

My Mother's Powder-compact

The powder
in my mother's powder-compact

smells of chalky gas
and makes me sick,

either on her neck
or on her shoes.

Sheep

They're streaming down the mountain
in their thousands

and crowding round my bed
where all night long

they stare into my eyes
as if to say

it isn't love I need:
it is *sheep*.

Loganberries

Strangers with sharp spades
have planted loganberries

on yellow canes
beside the shimmering lake

because they know
I pass this way to school,

and, knowing this,
they offer me their fruit.

Cat

I've found a dirty black-and-white cat
and wrapped it in a blanket like a pie

and force it to lie down with me and love me
but someone comes and drowns it in a bucket.

Summertime

Summertime
is like a hot tunnel

in which a scrum
of furious summer dresses,

all bunched-up and filthy,
thunders forward.

The Moon

It shines across the lawn.
It shines for me.

I know it does.
My mother knows it doesn't.

The Kiss

A fish
is said to live below the diving-raft

as big, or bigger,
than an elephant,

moving very slowly, if at all,
like something that belongs in a dream

where everyone is drowsy
and my mother

who in the dream is also not my mother
is being kissed for the first time.

Scar Tissue

It's what they call
"scar tissue" and it's shiny

and delicately blue
like an opal –

which is really nice
for, say, a wedding-dress,

but really stupid
for a person's head!

Fur

I'm running
like a frantic baby lake

running through the grass
to find its mother

because my skin
can't bear to feel the fur

that lives alone
inside the dead cat's basket.

I Never Put My Arms Round My Mother

I never put my arms round my mother
any more than any busy person

would stop
and put their arms round a mat

that's only there
in order to be trodden on

and trampled on – *stamp! stamp!* –
the more the better.

Our Life Together

The little things about our life together
make me feel sick – for example,

the way my mother likes to lay the table
(but nobody must ever know that).

Clock

My mother
is as deaf as the clock

above the bed
of someone who is screaming.

Heatwave

All afternoon
she sits beside the lake

underneath her large
and scratchy hat

waiting for the cows
to *go away*

that stand behind her,
breathing down her neck.

Bedtime

That my mother
can be loved

frightens me;
luckily

it frightens her too
and so she spends her days

out of sight
and lets me put *myself* to bed: *Goodnight!*

Word I'm Saying

Touch me
and I fall apart

like snow
that's much too warm

to hold itself together
(and if I speak

everything goes wrong
and no one understands a word I'm saying!)

The Horse

I used to be a girl
but gave it up

and grew my hair
and became a horse.

Lettuces

She purchases warm lettuces
from bungalows

loaded with red flowers
then hurries home,

dodging
the demented little Westies

that throw themselves
against her beige shins.

Jesus

No one comes to visit her in hospital
or visit me

because we've got no friends.
Jesus

is supposed to be our friend
but actually He doesn't even know us!

My Veins

I'm squatting on the tiles
in my dressing-gown

examining the veins
made by God

as part of His experiment
with pleasure.

People I Don't Like

Everything I say
is all wrong

and everything I do
makes her cry

and everything I see
I see through glass

where people I don't like
come peering in.

Sense

If I keep on getting so hysterical
they're going to have to lock me in my room

and fill the room chin-deep with damp sand
and leave me there until I *learn sense*.

Hook

I speak
and she is caught

like a fish.
Her lip is caught.

She finds
she can't look.

Stone

My head is bald and heavy
like a stone

a mother stone
is chipping into chippings.

When Mother Calls

When Mother calls
I dive into the lake

that knows that God is God
and calls Him ice.

Gloomy Ponds

The gloomy ponds
where fish as big as lorries

ply slowly up and down
ask no questions.

A Home She Loves

Although I am the size of a woman,
my mother is the size of a handkerchief

that seems to hover,
lacy and forlorn,

between a home she loves
and one she doesn't.

Penned Ewes

We're standing
back to back in the garden

like two penned ewes
who haven't got a flock.

My Hairy Legs

I used to be the size of a chicken
she used to feed with mashed scrambled egg

but now I am the size of a woman
and march about on thick hairy legs.

The Word for Love

She looks at me
like someone who can't look;

who wants to look but can't
and looks away;

who looks across the table
with a look

that seems to say
the word for love is *wall*.

Fresh Meat

My mother
is afraid of everything

and when she is afraid of things
she hums

and when she hums
I grow enormous breasts

that make her bedroom
smell of fresh meat.

Like Sombre Popes

Like sombre popes,
her golden eiderdowns

need to know
exactly what I'm doing.

The Little Suitcase

In the empty kitchen
boiled jam

drips and cools
beside the little suitcase

of someone who must leave
in a hurry.

A Woman's Hand

A woman's hand
is reaching for the hat

hanging in the hall
like an almond

that luckily
can neither see nor smell.

Chocolate

She crams it down her throat
like a murderess,

alone at last,
alternately *kissing* and *throttling*.

Mice

She doesn't know
she's trying to be happy;

she doesn't even know
who she is;

she only knows
that mice are running everywhere

whose tiny throats
can neither wheeze nor sing.

Dancing Days

She lies there
like a broken chandelier

that somebody has dressed
in a night-dress,

a chandelier
dreaming of her dancing days

when dancers were still gentlemen –
not *mice!*

Love Is What I Say

'Love' is what I say
but what I mean

is what if God could sin?
What if God

comes upstairs and opens my bedroom door
and stands beside my bed?

Or my mother's bed,
in which she lies bleeding and wheezing?

From What I've Seen

From what I've seen
and what I've heard

of love,
it's like a lake

on which you lie down:
I'm asking God

to show us how to do it,
how to love each other,

but
He won't!

Pain

The flies
and the descendants of the flies

overrun the garden
and the house

and have their babies
on the mats and mattresses

where everything that lives
lives in pain.

Pleasure

As if it was her only real pleasure
that now she has exhausted herself by,

she seems to have *stopped crying!*
and just glares;

her handkerchiefs
harden like fins.

Tick Tick Tick

Listen to the bars of the fire
cooling in the dark below her bed:

it makes a sort of ticking noise
like snow

falling on a woman
with sore ears.

Her Hands Against Her Ears

How wrong I was
to think I could just stand there

and scream and shout
as loudly as I could –

I screamed and shouted at her till she died,
her hands against her ears. End of story.

NYLON

for Betty

What My Northern Aunts Say

They say there's something wrong
with my brain,

they say they're sorry
but they say I'm sick,

they say I'm sick
but, sick or not, they say

the way I treat my mother's
inexcusable;

they say she thinks she's fine
but she's *not*!

Never mind,
I can go to hell

where women in white uniforms
are waiting for me.

Tobacco

The world is full
of nasty-looking people

who lie in wait
for people like ourselves

but all the same
we must soldier on,

the smell of their tobacco
notwithstanding.

Hospital

The fish that flicker
up and down the fish tank

do not know
how sad and thin they are;

they flicker here and flicker there
like thoughts

that do not know
who it is who's thinking them.

The South

I'm going to live with Bobby,
my new aunt,

who lives, the doctor tells me,
in The South

which means she wears
a cockatoo-print housecoat

and peep-toe mules
that smell of baby powder

and dances wild dances
on hot sand

with friends who drink like fish
and live on boats,

their skin as brown and thick
as buccaneers;

well greased by Cyclax,
slapped on every night

in bedrooms overrun
by bouncy poodles

as fragrant as camellias
and begonias;

I'm going to live with Bobby,
in the South,

and not the aunts
who live in the North

and live and die in darkness,
eating roots.

Sugar

I'm the girl
who makes her mother cry

(she cries and cries
until she can't stop!)

but Bobby doesn't care:
She thinks it's funny!

She gives me sugar necklaces
to suck on

and sings to me
as if she's going to explode!

Ashtray

Every time she stubs
her cigarette out

she chinks a shiny nail
against the glass;

even when she's naked
she does it –

yellow fingers,
lipstick on the butt.

Turkey Sandwiches

The seven French – or 'Standard' –
chocolate poodles

that Mr Biscuit's here
to clip and trim

are far away
beyond the lily pond

enjoying Mr Biscuit's
turkey sandwiches

and no amount of whistling
and hallooing

is going to get them
trotting back again.

Summer Dresses

When she sees
my row of summer dresses

she laughs enough
to raze entire jungles!

Small Children

She doesn't like small children
one bit

but Bobby knows
she's got to like *me*

and actually she *does!*
It's amazing!

I do whatever I want
and so does she:

many hours are spent
on the terrace

lying in the sun
with the dogs

and, when the sun goes down,
in the drawing-room,

feeding Charlie
cubes of orange melon.

The Girl in the White Vinyl Mini-skirt

She's talking to a man
who's got a poodle

that's *desperately*
in need of a home

and, all the time they're standing there
and talking,

I'm dancing
in a white vinyl mini-skirt

trimmed with mink
up and down the hall.

Snowflake

I call him that
after the gorilla –

although he isn't nearly
as nice:

he comes into my room
and eats my dresses

and drags my doll around
by her hair

and that's why I
don't like him anymore

but Babs and Mr Biscuit
just say *Tough*.

Airing-cupboard

I spent a lot of time
in the airing-cupboard

which may have been
a bit of a mistake

but I was very happy
in my cupboard,

very snug,
like a large fieldmouse.

Beetles

One or twice I'd hear
the crunch of footsteps

as someone walked away
across the gravel

but nothing else disturbed
the sound of beetles

making nests
inside my musty hair.

Trying Not to Think About My Mother

It's evening
and I'm playing on the terrace

trying not to think about
my mother

when seven poodles
leap into my lap

and bounce about
like seven clipped jacuzzis!

My Chocolate Cake

Another 'Auntie' soon arrives –
by boat! –

(smelling rather strongly
of fish!)

who marches up the shingle
crushing cockle-shells

then strides into the house
and eats my cake.

Aunt Bobby's Kitchen

Everything is blue
like fitted water

but stretchy – as if seen
from a trapeze –

and everyone is dressed
in almost nothing

like people made of sunlight
dresses as terns.

Aunt Bobby's Toaster

It likes to fling
its gold-encrusted slices

high into the air
like top C's

which silver spoons,
polished till they squeal,

load with her voluptuous-looking
strawberries.

You Can't Just Leave Her

They say
you can't just leave her

but she can!
She leaves me in a boat

with a poodle
who spends the day

pretending he's a lamb –
a lamb that swims,

that's taught himself
to can-can,

that thinks he's much too grand
to simply bleat

(but will, in certain circumstances,
yap);

a denizen of snow-bound
virgin forests

where growly bears and wild fairies
roam –

'and if he starts his
jumping-up tricks, poppet,

the thing to do is knee him,'
and I do!

Dawn

Still dreaming of a woman
like my mother

who keeps on falling,
getting up and falling,

I come downstairs at dawn
in my dressing-gown

to help myself
to Bobby's succulent chocolates.

Smile

She smiles at me
like a warm tureen

who's finding it's
too boring to talk.

Sausages at Dawn

She offers me a sausage
in a puddle.

This is not the way
we eat at home.

At home we eat
subtly-flavoured vegetables

dressed (like wounds!)
in subtly-flavoured sauces.

The Letter

Bobby says
Why not write a letter –

Say how good I've got
at making fairy cakes

or maybe something nice
about the sandals –

but can't she see
the dogs are getting restless?

Can't she hear their yapping?
Yes, she can:

out we go – *yap, yap* –
into the sunshine!

That shines on us
because it loves us so!

(But doesn't shine
on those who are sick.)

And do I ever write the letter?
No.

To writing, talking, thinking, I say
No.

Chou-Chou

'Chou-Chou' sounds so chic
and ballerinas

call each other *Chou-Chou*
all the time...

Could Baby be half-French?
I'm also wondering

could Baby in some way
be a man?

Pyjamas

Bobby pops her head
into the bathroom

and passes me
a pair of new pyjamas

still folded in their box
like pyjamas

made of soft, defrosting
apricots.

Mole

When I first arrived
from the city

where nothing could be seen
except walls

I blinked at people
like the humble mole

stunned by brightness,
but my heart was breaking.

Coffee

Her lips and nails blaze
like gladioli spikes

that know exactly
what it is they want

as down she plunges
on her silver plunger,

down into her frothy
coffee jug.

Poodle-Man

Here he is again,
Aunt Bobby's poodle-man,

sitting in the kitchen
eating bourbons

and laughing – what a laugh! –
with Aunt Bobby

who lolls beside him
like a bloated queen

eating more – much more –
than is good for her,

a woman who is naturally
so slender,

a *human greyhound*
Mr Biscuit says,

but Bobby just poo-poos him,
and chuckles,

and lobs another bourbon
at old Coco

who's feeling much too sick
to respond.

Baby in a Mackintosh

I'm sitting in the tree-house
licking Wagon Wheels

when Baby comes along
in a mackintosh –

singing
in what sounds like broken German

as if she's just emerged
from the sea

after having walked all night
through water,

her mouth chock-full
of chocolate-drops and cockle-shells –

and when she sees me staring down
she winks!

What She Cooks

What she cooks
is so completely different.

And normal women
lock the bathroom door.

Toot-toot

As soon as Mr Biscuit
toots his horn

they scamper off –
like disobedient hedges

with amber eyes
and liver lips and eye-rims

and nails that peep out
like black shrimp!

Small Birds

I used to live in darkness
like the mole

but now I walk about
completely normally

and as I walk about
I see smiles

fly about the room
like small birds.

Kitten

While Baby chop-chop-chops
the yellow lemon

for her and Bobby's
morning G-and-T,

she lets me take the last
half-melted kitten

whose chocolate lips
have never learnt to mew.

Aunt Bobby's Glasses

Her glasses
have strange points

like jewelled perches
that seem to be inviting

small parrots
firstly to alight

and then to rest
there.

Thinking About My Mother

We do not know, of course,
what she is thinking

as hour after hour
she lies in bed,

with nobody to talk to
but the beetles

that scuttle up and down
the empty wards;

we do not know
if she's awake or dreaming;

and, if she's dreaming,
if she dreams of me.

Kenny

When he finds her
chomping on my goose

and getting *drool*
and *kapok* everywhere,

Mr Biscuit –
I can call him Kenny –

distracts her
with a nice warm fishcake.

Night Would Fall...

Night would fall
and in the empty dining-room

I'd sit and watch
the beetles in their thousands

climbing up the wall
and falling off again...

I say she used to leave me there
all night!

but Bobby only laughs and says
she couldn't have!

Two Shimmering Aunts and a Goose

Even now – and look,
it's long past midnight –

they shimmer
like two elegant bouquets

as side by side
they sink into my eiderdown

and *promise* me
they'll mend it in the morning.

Large Blue

The sky's the colour of a large
Large Blue

God is in the process
of uncrumpling

and soon the yellow sun
will be blazing

and nothing else will matter
except *moisturiser.*

Matching Bathing-costumes

Although we mostly wear
our matching bathing-costumes

(except that Bobby's got
foam cups in hers –

like summer puddings
squashed against her boobies!)

sometimes we just wear
our ordinary knickers.

Crossing the Desert with a Pram

Nearly every night
I see the woman

walk across the desert
with her pram,

never getting closer,
or clearer,

and never getting further
away.

My Peacherino

Bobby,
like a fish in gold chains,

her glasses like gold fins,
her whole body

encrusted
in a suit of precious jewels,

glittering and spiky,
grabs my arm

and drags me to the boathouse
where my goose

is waiting in the boat –
my peacherino!

What We Like

What we like, we like,
they seem to say,

and what we don't
we just ignore; it's easy;

it's easy
to sit playing cards together

in summer evenings
when the days are long

and boats at anchor
tinkle as they sway.

Coco

When Mr Biscuit's bright pink van
appears

and two young men
lay Coco in the back,

no one sees me
running to the boathouse,

taking all the chocolate rabbits
with me:

we've always known
we've got to be this brave,

replacing being his
with being me,

huddled in a nest
of blue rope

inhaling the familiar smell
of turpentine.

Forgiveness

She loves to do
what she loves to do

and what she doesn't love
she doesn't do!

She doesn't make me
sit and chew my food,

she doesn't spend her days,
like my mother,

trying to find
the loneliest place on earth;

she doesn't stay at home
'to make the beds'

instead of going sailing
with the poodle man;

and doesn't care two hoots
about 'forgiveness'

because, my dear,
there's nothing to forgive!

Lip

A one-legged baby
made of brown rubber

is sitting on my lap
looking glum

while Bobby,
in her cockatoo-print house-coat,

dabs her lip
with dampened cotton-wool.

Bobby Looking Hot

Bobby looks as hot
as a mermaid

basted with the juices
of stewed fruit,

roasted till she smells
of steaming fish,

then propped outside the kitchen
while the cooks

go and fetch a knife
to slice her breasts with.

Jelly

Babs and Bobby
neither know nor care

what it feels like
to be unhappy –

what they care about
is shaking jelly

vigorously
out of jelly moulds

previously dipped
in boiling water.

Birthday Party

She thinks she looks dramatic
and she does –

her heels so high,
her hair so alarmingly red –

and when the puffed-out poodle-man
turns up

she treats us all to a deafening
Barbara Allen,

then Babs come bursting in
and announces

everyone is needed
at the boathouse!

Charlie's Girlfriend

When God made Charlie
He said 'Listen, Charlie,

soon I will be sending you
a girlfriend

and when you see her
you must *shriek at her*

and grab her by the hair
and then lean in

and peck her on the cheek
until she pouts

and starts to make
peculiar little *kissing-noises*

and this will mean *she loves you*!'
And I do!

I let him pinch the raisins
from my fruitcake

and hide them for him
in my ears and hair.

Art

Mr Biscuit's so-called
'works of art'

are busy getting duckshit
on their pom-poms

while choosing to ignore
Mr Biscuit

who's running round the lawn
squeaking squeaky things.

Warble-fly

Now what's going on!
Here comes Baby

prancing up the lawn
like a warble-fly

looking for a juicy wound
to trample in.

Magnolia

Coco,
once so warm to the touch,

lies in mud
beneath the white magnolia

planted for him
by the late opera-singer.

Finch

It's lying on the sofa
wet with blood

and asking why I hate it –
when I *don't* hate it!

Bobby in the Bathroom

What does Bobby
do in there, I wonder;

and why's she hiding currants
in his cardigan?

and can you catch a goldfinch
with an oven mitt?

and what I want to know is
is it true

unhappiness
is just a waste of tissue-paper?

Ballerinas

A corps of tissue-paper
ballerinas

gathers in my room
like ballerinas

that gather
in some shady lagoon

in order to be taught
how to honk.

Shopping

Bobs and Bobby,
snug in tartan trews,

their lips as red as blood,
are going shopping –

leaving me and Snowflake
on the river

that ripples like a river
wrapped in ocelot.

Charlie

When Mr Biscuit's
freshly clipped poodles

go rushing past his perch
and wake him up,

he screams at Mr Biscuit
like a banshee

then shits
on all his precious sprays and clippers.

After Dinner

After dinner –
long after dinner –

I think I hear Aunt Bobby
play the flute,

or someone playing something,
and the poodles,

understanding nothing,
come upstairs

and nibble me
like blunt-ended scissors.

Poodles of the Late Opera Singer

Ghostly
in the early morning mist,

the seven poodles
of the late opera singer

are fanning out across the lawn
to wee.

Cup-cakes

Baby and Bobby,
brown as chocolate cup-cakes,

watch me push the dinghy
out to sea

where all day long
the sun beats down like honey

on shoulders that could easily
so easily! –

bear aloft
my little bony mother,

disintegrating
in the City hospital

like someone's arm
inside an old lion.

Bobby at 3 P.M.

When Aunt Bobby
falls into the bathroom

she sees another Bobby
in the mirror,

and when she falls asleep
the other Bobby

slithers down
and falls asleep beside her.

Such Chic Pom-poms

Why are her belts so tight
she can hardly breathe

and why does she wear her dressing-gown
not done up

and why does she toss her head
like a spring chicken

and who is the man
she drinks with at *The Ship*

and is it true
unhappiness is pointless

and does she owe her happiness
to nakedness

and are they virgins in a way
or not

and could I too
give Snowflake such chic pom-poms

and has it got too late
to change my mind

and what do I think
and what do I see when I see

her pubic hair's
triangular wire-wool

and when is a woman a woman
and when's she a warble-fly

prancing up the lawn
spelling trouble?

Sunburn

Aunt Bobby's skin is screaming
as she gingerly

peels off
the elasticated bikini-top

she should have left upstairs
in my drawer

or in the airing-cupboard
where I left it.

Eggs

The poodle in my bed –
who won't get off,

who looks at me
as if I'm not worth looking at;

as if I ought to know
she's now a bird,

and can't get off
because she's laying eggs,

as if she's disappointed in me –
blinks.

The Curtain

My cache of sticky
barleysugar sticks

the man who gave me Snowflake
used to give me

is hidden
at the back of my drawer

to stop the poodles
getting hold of it

and crunching it to bits
until the lino

glitters
like the dashboard of the Riley

I'm driven in
to buy my first bra,

but first I have to go
behind a curtain,

(actually a sheet)
above the hardware shop,

(a nylon sheet
the colour of icy metal)

where everything
including my first bra

smells of the man who runs the shop's
tobacco.

Mint Imperials

The *Mint Imperial* mints
I get from Kenny

roll about
among my vests and knickers

like tiny emu eggs
the emu mothers

must have left behind
in a rage

when off they went
to learn the art of kicking

but late last night
I heard them at my door:

sick of fighting seamstresses
and milliners,

limping and undone,
they had come back –

but I was tired
and didn't let them in

and as I drifted off
I heard one say

how *miserable*
their evenings had become

now that there was no demand
for empresses.

Desert Dew

The woman with white hair
like my mother's

who pushes her black pram
across the desert

is pushing it
more and more slowly

as if her little arms
are getting weaker,

or else her load
is somehow getting heavier,

but heavier than what?
with desert dew?

or could the woman
be collecting something?

(but what can one collect
in a desert?)

or could she have
what used to be a baby,

and what is now a child,
that she pushes,

its flabby body
strapped inside the hood?

For all we know,
the body in the pram

is bigger
than the woman herself!

(I call the body 'body'
and not 'person'

because it's in a dream
and in a dream

people are just heaps
without names...)

My Last Goodnight

I've said my last goodnight
to the poodles,

and closed my eyes,
and everything goes black:

black, the snow-white dresses,
black, the snow;

black, O black,
the crystal chandelier;

black the night
in which my snow-white mother

dances
as she's never danced before.

Maple Brazils

She's passing me some sweets
'for the train' –

the kind I like,
Maple Brazils –

and saying
there'll be someone there to meet me

and take me to the house
and I say *fine*.

Privacy

I'm sitting on the train
with my bags

and, on my shoulders,
like a bag, my head

in whose dark tunnels
lurks my monster brain

that – unlike sweets? –
won't let itself be touched;

that – unlike Bobby's sweets! –
needs its privacy

in which to plot
its terrible revenge.

The House

When I'm at the house
I will invite

as many standard poodles
as I can

to come upstairs
and pile on my counterpane

and weigh me down
and squash me

till I'm blue
and can't remember how to take breaths.

Icy Metal

Icy metal
sticks to their skin,

the moisture in their nostrils
starts to freeze

as, step by step,
my cruel northern aunts,

late, O never late,
for a train,

sally forth
across benighted lawns

crunchy with the chains
and bones of truckers

kept alive
on boiled horses' heads

but only for so long,
they die of cold,

dreaming of crude oil
and rough diamonds,

their eyes wide open,
hearts as cold as flowers

bulky truckers
heading north to nowhere,

to settlements
too dark and cold for sweethearts,

inhabited by nothing
but the wind,

and, bent against the wind,
my northern aunts

who live on lumps of root
and boiled children.

BUNKER SACKS

1

Mother can't go on like this much longer:
Mother's made a terrible mistake!
Let's hope this baby grows up nice and fast!
She wants – *she needs* – to get back to that office.
She needs her tidy desk and all her things,
she needs to go and sit herself down
and tuck her chestnut hair behind her ear

and do her work – *get on with her work!* –
What's wrong with that? Too bad about the baby!
Anyway it's tough as old boots –
and getting tougher – isn't that right, Baby?

2

Someone's propped it up on a mat
where all day long it yells for its rabbit
but someone's much too busy in the scullery
holding ice against her rock-hard breasts
to run around picking up rabbits
here, there and everywhere for people
who spend all day underneath one's feet,
rolling around on the floor dribbling and widdling.

3

It thinks the world is absolutely hilarious!
The cherry-blossom on the pram? Hilarious!
The greenish-yellow pond like liquid goose-shit?
its mother's pain? Hilarious! hilarious!

4

They pull their heavy boots on: hey, let's go!
It makes them feel sick just to look.
There must be somewhere else – a proper city
where people can be people, and make phone calls,
and breathe the air God meant them to breathe.
These handsome men can't really be expected
to function in a houseful of cows.

5

First of all it needs to understand
that all it does is get in people's way
and nothing it can do will change a thing
and nobody will ever be its friend.

6

The women, I am sorry to say,
crawl around feeling sick, and gasping,
as if the air was gas. They gasp and croak.
No wonder these brave men are setting off
to find a place where air is air for once,
men who have no faults, dynamic men,
men who are so tall they can't quite hear,
far below them, shaky voices calling.

7

She's tired of feeling choked all the time –
as if there's someone jumping on her chest
(while outside in the sunlight the baby
really *is* choking! On cherry blossom!)

8

It's easy not to love and not to eat,
to join the line that snakes across the mountains
towards a world where air
is breathed in deeply;
it's easy to abandon small children
that seem to be already bald and dead.

9

The baby calls for somebody to come.
By 'calls' I mean it bawls.
But no one comes.
What a shame! Everyone is sick!
Sickness like a huge rubber mouth
is going round *breathing* on everybody.

10

Waking from a dream of small children
tucked between her thighs like anemones,
the woman watches as a line of ants
drags their creamy eggs across the baby
and down a sandy hold beside its head
where nurses in red uniforms are waiting for them.

11

It's easy to be easy when it's easy,
the air is air, the mothers rock blue prams
and chuckle as the frothy drifts of blossom
drift across their motherly laps –
but now, the slightest thing and they're gasping,
they seem to give up hope and die like flies.
Lift the sack and see for yourself!
Goodness knows how long they have been lying here!
Some of them have even got their babies,
still wrapped in awkward bandages and masks.

12

Grey against the glaring yellow sky,
a woman with a pram can be seen
making her slow way down the bank
where bugs and beetles dream their tiny dreams.

13

Each lung is like a lung crushed by Spandex
in preparation for eternity!

14

Long ago, before she was a woman,
when she was a girl, older women
offered her a dress, to make her beautiful;
they shouted *Put it on*, *Put it on*,
they flapped their crimson fingers and they promised her
that *everyone would love her*! – but they didn't.

15

It comes at night and squeezes her
like rubber,
it crushes her until she can't breathe,
it clamps onto her lips with such force
it forces kisses out of her like shit.

16

She likes to trap stray dogs and boil them
and give the boiled bones to the baby
who sucks and gnaws at anything you give it
(which is very gratifying, isn't it?)

17

The handbag where she kept her contraceptives
now contains a nest of golden centipedes
that glitter in the pocket of the lining
like toffees in the hands of the sick.

18

It likes to chaw her nipples till she cries
and then it likes to chaw at them some more.
Look, it wants to chaw her all night long!
Her chestnut hair hangs down across her face
and sticks to it like streaks of blood to concrete.

19

Insects file past into the forest
and, as they pass, the baby intercepts them.
Some of them get tortured, others killed.
Stop messing around and go to sleep for Chrissake!

20

Just because it yowls at her like that
it doesn't mean to say she has to *throttle* it –
that's not very motherly, now is it?
Of course, she doesn't really throttle it!
She dumps it in a yard of old carts
then crawls into the bunker again –
which nearly throttles *her* it's so foggy!

21

Off it wobbles, scraping its fat knees...
You're going to have to learn to *get up*, Baby!
(It doesn't know the bridges have collapsed;
it doesn't know the roads are getting stonier...)

22

The baby likes to sleep with its rabbit
who likes to tell it how to live with moths
in realms of gold where grey exhausted mothers
dip their nipples into bowls of ice.

23

Warm and spongy like a little cake –
and, like a little cake, attracting flies –
who, I wonder, could have left it here,
its tiny heart thumping and thumping?

24

The little rabbit hops,
deranged but cheerful,
out across the sand
to the lake
and hops into the water
where it drowns
and sinks into the mouths of wriggly fishes.

25

The baby's like a bag full of oil
with nothing to befriend it
but the light
whose yellow hands
keep pushing it around,
forcing it to whimper and squint.

26

It's taking its first steps –
O how adorable!
It doesn't ever want to crawl again!
Off it goes towards the yellow lake,
its dirty feet bleeding as it goes.
You think it's going to wobble in – but no,
it finds a nice, smooth rock to go to sleep on
and goes to sleep (like on a baking tray!)

27

Everyone is sick but the baby:
the baby hasn't finished living yet!
It hasn't had enough of being satisfied –
of shitting, sucking and of being sucked.

28

They gather in the branches of the trees
and wait in rows like birds for the end.
The sick remain below like sleepy pears,
some in sacks, some in sandy hollows.

29

It cries until you think it can't go on
then suddenly it rises to its feet
and staggers off once more across the rubble,
its tiny toes as dusty as a bun,
though why it keeps on going no one knows,
or anyway no one can explain ...
it keeps on going like a little bun
that's got a little key in its bottom!

30

The baby's sick, it stinks of shells and cheeses.
In the quarry, fallen ponies rot.
Summer's gone and won't be coming back:
it's absolutely sick and tired of everybody!

31

Does this woman know or doesn't she
the simple word, the simple concept, *discipline*?
Whipping, thumping, whacking? Can't she see
you owe it to a baby! After all,
it's better to be dead than grow up whingeing.

32

Let's knee it in the chest!
Quite right too!
And send it yowling back into the bunker.
Has it ever thought (no, it hasn't!)
that *it* could humour *her*, for a change?
Another thing,
who does God make babies?
What's *that* all about?
I've no idea!

33

It cries so much it's starting to go blue
but no one's here to grab it and whack it
and tell it it must *stop*. Too bad.
It quivers in the gloom until its drool
makes rivulets across the sandy tunnel.

34

It looks as if the baby might survive –
anyway for a few days.
And when I say a *few* I mean a *few*
so if you're going to love it, love it *now*!
What she needs is grace but unfortunately
we don't know what it is, or where to find it.
(It sounds so nice, doesn't it – 'grace'? –
but actually it's making her distraught!)

35

It used to have a pram to fall asleep in.
It used to have a pillowcase to suck at.
Today it's lying down in the snow.
It thinks the snow is fun! – but it's not.

36

From the hills a pair of sunken eyes
watch the woman walk into the forest
but nobody has noticed the baby staggering along the top bank
then dropping down beside the yellow rushes –
Being still is simple but not easy ...
The hungry wolf comes down the path to drink.

37

Although she's much too bony to be cute,
I have to say this woman breaks your heart –
or would if there were any hearts to break! –
this woman and her dressing-gown of flies
crawling blindly down the dank tunnel.
Where the hell's she crawling off to anyhow?
It makes you sick the way she gropes and slobbers.

38

Now it's smearing shit along the wall,
its lips and fingers bald as newborn mice.
It isn't looking good, is it? Please,
does it have to shit all the time?

39

When it gets far out in the open
the baby falters,
and it snows again;
the woman swings her axe
one last time,
takes a piece of wood
and goes inside
and deepest night returns to the valley,
stealing down the bank on dusty paws.

40

Everything is damp and nothing burns
and in the farthest corner of the bunker
she's staring into space like an extra
waiting to perform as the moon.

41

The baby's on the floor of the tunnel
picking at the crust round its eye:
winter is not meant for little babies!
Beneath the bunker even rats decay.

42

Today the last surviving birds of prey
watch her put the baby in a sack
and roll the little sack – there it goes! –
down into the echoing ravine...
(Which of us hasn't sometime peered
down into a similar ravine
and watched the easy river far below
shimmer in its bed of rocks and fish-bones?)

43

If she wants to dies she can die;
if she wants to sin she can sin:
this woman's feeling better already!
She likes it here. Yes, it's very peaceful...

44

Before it died,
she heard the baby speak!
(although of course she couldn't have – I mean
that baby never learnt to say anything!)

45

She tells the little body she'll be down –
to bury it underneath a rock –
but then – how sad! – (it happens all the time) –
in the end she never does go down.

46

That night the woman dreams she wears the dress
the other women said would make her beautiful.
As soon as people saw her, they would love her!
Love! At long long last!... But they didn't.

47

Whoever built the bunker must be dead,
resting in the heavens where the planets
are tired of going round and round and round
and wish a rest could be arranged for *them*!

48

Ghostly birds suddenly take flight
and flap their way across the frozen valley
where far below a woman can be heard
calling, calling for her lost Leghorn.

49

The woman inches forward on all fours.
Could someone be alive? I don't think so!
The cave is empty but the dust is warm.
Now all she needs is a pair of bedroom slippers!

50

Because they told her everyone would love her
she put it on – but nobody did love her!

51

The bunker sacks
darken with black tears
that don't know what they're doing
they're so wet.

52

Long ago she had a pair of shoes
she sang to sleep at night like frightened children
and now she wishes she had shoes again –
a pair of shoes to sing to *her* this time!

53

Put it on, they shouted, *put it on!*
but when she put it on they disappeared.

54

A lorryload of toddlers in gold trainers
is tethering her corpse to a tree.
Her yellow dress in weighed down by mud;
the yellow grass is weighed down by shit.
Like every mother that has ever lived,
she wants to look her best at all times!
If she's got to be a corpse, she begs them,
let her be a corpse dressed in pink –
pink be-jewelled jodhpurs, pink jacket,
and a pair of pink, unwearably-high high-heels!
Actually this woman's now so thin
she's like a little crust of sand... it's pitiful...
we know we must not hurt our dear mothers:
we certainly must never hurt this one!

Any minute now she'll fall apart.
Luckily for her, she doesn't know that:
when she sees a river, in she leaps;
when she sees a mountain, up she hikes,
when she sees – or thinks she sees – a man,
she guzzles at him like there's no tomorrow!
(Which actually there isn't!) That's better.
She doesn't understand a single thing
but isn't that so sweet? You won't believe this
but far away she thinks she hears a pony.
Far away the little jingly pony either is or isn't on its way;
far away the blood that drips from Jesus
either does or doesn't drip for *her*.)

55

Because they promised *everyone would love her*
she put it on and did up all the buttons
and stepped outside and walked across the lawn
in matching shoes. But did they love her? No.

56

She walks about like someone in a cage,
determined not to cry, her big blue tears
welling up inside her throat like trout.
Being brave is such a waste of time!
If only there were cities still standing;
if only there were buildings, and a room;
if only she were standing in the room
while dressmakers of every description
kneel at her feet with pins (like toddlers
who cram their mouths with crunchy ants and beetles!)

57

Insects in bow-ties and bow-trim loafers
are waving at her from the dark woods
and those that have located her blood
are tucking in in violent jerky sucks.

58

Now the woman thinks she's a weasel!
Can't she understand (no, she can't)
that everything alive is now dead?
Anyway a weasel's not worth eating.
(She might as well make love to a centipede!)

59

She's like a little song-bird she's so small
– a songbird that refuses to sing!
(She still assumes that everyone will sneer at her
even though there's no one her to sneer at her!
She seems to think there's still a city somewhere,
a city with a dressmaker in it;
she even think this last surviving dressmaker
is going to 'run her up' a pink dress
in which she'll storm the last surviving night-club
and fuck the last surviving man to death!)

60

Still the bony woman struggles on.
She digs for roots. She grunts. And then she falls.
And grunts again. And then she disappears,
scuttling into shadows like a spider.

61

Grove, I said, not *grave*... that cough again...
And now look what she thinks she's found:
a dressing-gown!

62

She waves her arms around in the dark
feeling for... for what?... a little something?
(Not a human being, obviously –
She knows it's much too late for one of *them*!)

63

Wear this dress, they said,
and we will love you,
this scratchy and asphyxiating dress.
Wear it, wear it, wear it, so she wore it.
They turned towards her but forgot her name.

64

It's easy to be weak when you're weak;
to gasp; to never hope, no matter what;
it's easy to bung crystals up your nose,
to shuffle through the mountains with no light,
to never reach the pass, to have no name,
to wear the dress that men will rape you in,
and batter you, and no amount of anything
will ever make you feel right again.

65

She thinks she can't go on – but she can!
Concentrate on your breathing exercises!
Breathing, did you say? You must be joking!
She needs to concentrate of being dead.

66

It's easy to be guilty when you're guilty,
it's easy to be sick when you're sick,
it's easy to be sad when you're lonely –
and it's easy to be dead when you're dead!

67

The women from the mountains find the sack
lying in the sun against a rock
but nothing would induce them, they agree,
putting down their sacks, to eat a *baby*.

68

The women who would never eat a baby –
that they have agreed – continue on.
Don't they know that after this grey valley
there's going to be another grey valley?

Yes, they do. But to continue on,
against all odds, is easier than stopping;
easier than rotting in the heat;
easier than being torn apart
by women from the mountains with no manners,
women who have roamed the gloomy valleys
for many days and nights without food,
who when they see it rotting in its sack
fall on it and tear it apart;
who don't know what they're doing they're so happy,
who look around,
who see each other's lesions,
who – wait a minute!... can this be right? –
proceed to tear *each other* apart!

69

Actually what happens next is this:
when they see it rotting in its sack
they fall on it and hack it to bits
and strip the little body till it's bone
and then they look around – this can't be right –
and start to hack *each other* to bits!
No wonder that poor woman we began with
wanted to get back to her office,
to people who are cool and relaxed,
smiling in their air-conditioned air.

GRUNTER

My Mother

Don't say she doesn't try! Of course she does!
She tries and tries. She never stops trying.
She tries until she thinks her heart will break.
But nothing works: I am unlovable.

The Cot

The cot I'm all tucked up in catches fire
but never mind! In a few months,
still alive but now no longer whole,
I'm back at home (if you can call it home!)
but now they know that something isn't right,
but what it is or isn't no one knows,
they only know that, if I am a person,
I'm not a person in the way that they are.
I sat and burned in silence, for example.
And still, age one, I 'fail to reach out'.

Furniture Polish

When I'm three they send me to a convent.
My head is large but it doesn't matter.
I like to stroke the crust on Jesus' blood,
and sniff the Sisters' furniture polish.

Happiness

I'm wet and cold and happy but my mother
thinks I should be very *unhappy*
and calls me in in words like melted butter
laced with pins to *come and get dry.*

Lump

Why do I just sit here like a lump
and let myself be hit all afternoon?
And why am I still here, six hours later,
pouring blood and rigid? No one knows.
One of them pokes me with a stick.
I ought to be removed. I'm disgusting.

Egg

I don't know which way up I am in space
or where space is
or if it ever ends
or why it's taken all my words away
or why she says I can when I can't
and why, when I'm supposed to be so brainy,
why am I so dim I can't reply,
I can't, I won't,
her voice is like an egg
running from the corners of her mouth –
it's running over here –
get away!

A Silver Ball

A silver ball the size of a pea
balances on the silver frame
that frames the mirror where the doctor sits
sucking on a mint whose silver foil
I saw him peel when I left the room.

The Hand

The hand that reaches out
is my mother's
and I refuse to touch it and the water
once again closes over me.

Glass

If anybody touches me I shatter
and bits of glass go everywhere like beeps.
The doctor says *I'm sorry*. I am too.
I'm sorry I can't hear a word he's saying.
I'm sorry I can't stop repeating sorry.
I'm sorry if I'm sorry. I'm a genius.
I'm sorry if I'm sick. *You can go.*

Boxes

I mustn't spin.
I mustn't push my eyeballs in.
I mustn't duck when people try and touch me.
I mustn't sleep with boxes on my face
or chew my arm or lick the bathroom wall
and even in my dreams I must never
ride around bareback. (I'm a girl!)

Synonyms

The others give the answers teachers want:
I only give the answers that are right.
When they say to pick the pairs of words
that mean the same, I always answer *none*.

My Mother's Tongue

When her voice sounds runny like this
it means she wants to kiss me –
and my world
turns not only upside-down but yellow:
even her long tongue is bright yellow!

Pear

The cubes of pear mustn't touch the sausage slices,
the sausage slices mustn't touch the pear.
(By 'mustn't' I mean if they do I scream,
by 'scream' I mean they wish *I was dead*!)

I Don't Like Who They Are

I don't like who they are
or what they want
or what they may or may not say or do
but there's one thing I like them for a lot –
for chess! (For chess, they will – and do – sit still.)

The Cupboard

Sitting in a cupboard is depressing:
if he were me, *he* would be depressed!
But can't he understand it's me who's me
sitting in the cupboard? And *I* like it!

The Wedding

Everybody else is drinking wine.
I have to look as if I understand.
I have to understand I must sit down.
And when the food arrives, I must eat it.

Mud

Out I go, tearing off my bridesmaid's dress,
and roll myself around in the mud
and then I have run like the wind
back into my room before they catch me
but on the way I bump into a rabbit
as big as the hotel who's peering in,
right into the room where the speeches are,
its furry jowls pressed against the glass,
but nobody is taking any notice,
they're concentrating on their hats and cake slices.

Stugeron

I'm odd because I'm trying to be normal
not because I'm trying to be odd!
And why might I be trying to be normal?
So everyone will leave me alone
and let me live in peace in my cupboard
breeding rabbits made of Stugeron.

Praise

Being praised makes me feel sick.
It makes me feel no one wants to know
who I am or why I do the things
I try to do less well at or in secret.

The Dining-room

The dining-room is the perfect place
for making love in in the early morning
if you are a fly or a cook
or somebody who's in another world
and does not know what the cook is doing.

Podgy

I say he's looking *podgy*. That is rude.
He's looking *very podgy*. Also rude.
I do my best to stop myself from saying it
but then I say it one more time. *Podgy*.

My Mother's Dead

My mother's dead.
A spider has eight legs.
These are facts.
I love them very much.
The same for ever,
neutral as a clock.

Therapy

The therapist says to go outside
and bring back 'something beautiful to share'
so out I go and, seeing an old gardener,
bring him in, slung across my shoulder.

Perfect Order

No, I'm neither angry nor depressed.
I know they think I should be but I'm not.
Everything is fine in my cupboard,
the knots, the motes, the rays in perfect order.

The Girl

Because he knows I can't stand being touched,
the man I live with feeds me sleeping pills
and tucks me up to one side of the bed
and then another girl, who does like sex,
joins us later on the other side.
(And if I start to make my funny noises
he chucks a blanket over my head!)

The Tower

Love is like a tower with no doors
and mile after mile of gold passages
where somebody or something is waiting for me
who doesn't seem to know about the doors.

Polycotton

His polycotton tells me I will never
meet my god or find my true home.

Alexandra Palace

Somebody puts me in a corner
and tells me not to move, and I don't,
I curl inside the jackets on the floor
and never speak or even look up;
occasionally he takes me to the toilet
then disappears into the crowd again –
as if it comes so naturally! (It certainly
doesn't come naturally to *me*!)

My Hair

Everything flies past at top speed
and soon my hair starts hurting me again
and people start giving off the smell
people say I mustn't sniff or mention.

The Drawing-room

When they take me to the drawing-room
they make me feel like a wild animal –
and everything that a wild animal
does is wrong, wrong, wrong in a drawing-room!

Cube

The cube of ice in the tall glass
shimmers like a cube of tranquillity
in which I could be happy at last
if only God would show them how to purify me.

The Bench

I'll sit here on this bench and not move.
If anybody touches me I'll bite them.
Here comes someone now. In creaky boots.
Back, back, back! I only like rabbits.

Joy

I'm grunting now but soon I will be screaming:
I scream until the sky itself is screaming.
I scream for how I am.
I scream for joy.
There's only this one mouth in the universe,
only one, it's open, and it's mine.

Fun

I'm screaming at full blast and it's fun –
it's fun to slide head first down the stairs,
it's fun to not get ready for the party,
to watch the Rover pull away without me;
it's fun to only eat defrosting peas,
it's fun to be attacked by wasps and bees,
it's fun to leave the train when no one's looking
and be another person somewhere else;
it's fun to cover walls and floors with loops,
great loops of snot,
or loops of lines of Muscidae;
to have no friends, to read the dictionary,
column after column, all night long;
it's fun to wear my bra inside out,
to chew my arm, to dangle upsidedown,
to bang my great big head until it bleeds;
it's fun to bleed,
it's fun to eat dead flies,
it's fun to lie down naked in the snow
and feel snowflakes brush my lips and nipples,
to run and run round and round the house,
to run across the grounds to the road,
to run across the road to the river,
to nose around underneath the water,
to lie, rolled-up and wet, in someone's boat;
it's fun to rock a wolfhound in my lap
(so bony she digs holes in my belly!),
it's fun to be alone at night with God
who visits me in the form of lint.

Being *them*, however, sounds like hell.
I hear they feel cold when it's cold
and when they feel pain I hear it hurts
and other people – this I can't believe! –
other people are a comfort to them.
Very strange. They never comfort *me*.

Stars

I've never been so happy in my life!
I climb onto the parapet and leap –
witnessed by the stars in the sky
and by their chopped reflections in the river.

Grunter

Don't look at me as if you're always thinking
do I have to grunt – because I do!
Do I have to sit in here and grunt
and flap my hands like budgies?
Yes, I do!
I've got a lot of things I need to grunt about!
Don't tell me I must stop because I won't,
don't ask me what I mean – I mean everything!

And if my grunt offends you, hear my scream:
when I scream it's like I grab your head
and everything goes red and there is nothing,
absolutely nothing you can do
and please don't say there is
because there isn't
and please don't even think about approaching me
and never touch me: I am mine, all mine.

Some Facts Are Small

Some facts are small
and some are large
but all of them
are at my service for eternity.

Eternity

Eternity is like a plain or plateau
overrun by millions of rabbits
that weigh me down like rabbits made of flour
and never stop until they stop me breathing.
(Once when I was taken to the sea,
I swam away, still wearing my coat!
Another time, I left my so-called 'boyfriend'
fast asleep on a train to Italy
and found myself alone in the snow
somewhere in the middle of nowhere.
The only man I didn't leave was blind.
I liked the way *he had never seen me*.
I left that man as well in the end.
He passed the time by burning his fingertips.)

The Fly

He says he's going to hit me in a minute
and then he says I'm TRYING to be stupid
and then a fly flies past at top speed
and then he says he will and then he doesn't.

Rain

When he says 'we could go indoors'
I suddenly remember people do:
people like to go *indoors* to meet,
especially when it's pouring with rain!

The Meeting

He asks me what I'ld like to have to drink
but when his back is turned at the bar
I suddenly run off. I can't help it.
No one seems to know how to stop me.

The Three-legged Bird

I'm like a three-legged bird who roams the world
searching for another three-legged bird
and people always say there's no such thing
and what I'd better do is live with them
in one of their 'specially built' cages.

Rock

People think a rock doesn't cry.
Of course it does. It simply does it silently.

Space

They cannot seem to understand that love
makes my body fall apart like sand
and then I have to set off into space
to get it back together again!

Sex

The fact that they 'had sex!' doesn't interest me.
Sex, to me, is like the violin.

Comfort

People who need comforting will turn –
I've noticed this a lot – to other people.
This doesn't work for me. On the contrary,
it makes me feel worse, I'm afraid.

Thunder

It feels like I'm in an egg-and-spoon race
in which my egg is actually my brain:
I hold it out in front of me and tremble
as men with eggs in boxes thunder by!

My Condition

Because of 'my condition' we all know
I'm not the same as them but they pretend,
in order to be kind, that I am,
but then we get confused, because I'm not!

Sand

Now my friends have learnt not to touch me,
the next thing I must do is to explain
I do however like to be COMPRESSED!
(But *not by them*! It needs to be a *thing*.
A duvet full of sand for example.)

Home

The only home I think I know is fur
that comes and holds me when I close my eyes,
fur as black and cold as the lake
into which I never stop falling.

On Days Like This

On days like this I'm tempted to give in
and let them take me back to the hospital
where people sit about in monster slippers
trying to relax (it's very tiring!)
but anyway it really doesn't matter,
they only want to die, they won't hurt you.